Thank You for Being a Friend:
A Golden Girls Trivia Book
By
Michael D. Craig

Other Books by Michael D. Craig

Thank You For Being a Friend: A Golden Girls Trivia Book

Who's That Girl? The Ultimate Madonna Trivia Book

The Totally Awesome 80s Pop Music Trivia Book

The Totally Awesome 80s TV Trivia Book

Published by Five Apples Press

For Dorothy, Sophia, Rose and Blanche…
Thank you for being our friends…

And in memory of my beautiful and amazing
Aunt Marilyn Mershall…you are missed.

Table of Contents

Acknowledgements

My deepest appreciation to all of the following people for their help, support and encouragement to me during the writing of this book:

To all my family: Dad, Mom, Paula, Diane, Martin, Tony, Ashley and Jeremy.

My wonderful stepsister, Kim Carver, for being such a loyal supporter and friend to me.

My two incredible and beautiful Aunts, Wanda and Phyllis.

Samantha Feldwick, my pop culture compatriot and fellow Golden Girl enthusiast in Great Britain, and web master of www.thegoldengirlsuk.com, the best GG site on the Web.

My good friends at www.80sXchange.com

All my amazing and wonderful friends at the "JC": Susan, Lisa, Rodney, Linda, Carrie, Megan, Jeannette, Phyllis, Norvella, Orville, Rozella, Janice, Maggie, Diana, Annabelle, Polly and Mr. Dunagan.

And special thanks to my beloved Marka, Donna Graham and Arnie Spence, Angel, Tonya, Jodi, Joan, Sarah and Katie! I love and miss you guys so much!!!

Thank you for being my friend!

The Golden Girls

In 1985, an incredible group of actors, writers and producers came together to create one of the best-loved and most critically acclaimed television sitcoms of all time, *The Golden Girls*. Blessed by the astonishing chemistry between four amazingly talented actresses, Bea Arthur, Estelle Getty, Betty White and Rue McClanahan, the show was an immediate success, quickly winning over an entire generation of television viewers from around the world.

The show became a Top Ten staple on television, not just in the United States, but in countless other countries as well. The series showcased the lives of a group of woman, all over the age of fifty, dispelling myths of women's sexuality after menopause and proving that there was laughter to mine from the life of the mature, American woman. The show also tackled many controversial themes for the time, including homosexuality, euthanasia, AIDS, the plight of the homeless and racism, all without losing the trademark sense of humor that made the show so incredibly popular.

Each of the show's four actresses received countless award nominations and accolades for their brilliant performances on the show, and each one took home at least one coveted Emmy Award. The creators, writers and producers also received a lion's share of awards and nominations for their impressive efforts. *The Golden Girls* continued its success throughout the late-80s and into the 90s, keeping up with the changing times while continuing to be a hit with viewers. In 1992, Bea Arthur decided that it was time to move on from the comfortable nest of the program and opted to leave at the end of her contract. The creators and producers, knowing that a major part of the show's appeal would be missing without the presence of Bea, decided to end the show, after a successful seven year run, even though the show still had very high ratings. The show's final episode was shot, centering around the wedding of Dorothy to Blanche's Uncle Lucas. The series finale was touching, sentimental and funny, showing the hallmark of a truly great sitcom by balancing hilarity with great poignancy and tenderness. The end of an era had arrived.

In the fall of 1992, the writers and producers brought the three remaining actresses together again for a second show, a spin-off series titled *The Golden Palace*. Although the three actresses still possessed the same wonderful chemistry, the show failed to click with viewers and was cancelled after only one lackluster season.

Although *The Golden Girls* has been out of production for over thirteen years, the show has really never left the air. The Lifetime Television Network has snapped up the exclusive rights to broadcast *The Golden Girls* on their cable network in the US on a daily basis, to very high ratings. In fact, after *Seinfeld* and *Friends*, it is the highest rated syndicated sitcom on cable television! The show is also in syndication in countless countries around the globe, winning over an entire generation of new fans that were infants or not even born during the show's initial run. This guarantees that *The Golden Girls* will live on, growing in popularity well into the new millennium!

Thank You for Being a Friend: The Golden Girls Trivia Challenge

<u>Multiple Choice</u>

1. Where did Sophia live before moving in with the Girls?
   (A) Rolling Hills
   (B) Shady Pines
   (C) Sicily
   (D) Brooklyn

2. From the list below, who **DID NOT** make a guest appearance on the show?
   (A) Julio Iglesias
   (B) Bob Hope
   (C) Burt Reynolds
   (D) Don Johnson

3. What was Blanche's maiden name?
   - (A) Hollingsworth
   - (B) O'Hara
   - (C) Rosenfeld
   - (D) Devereaux

4. Which celebrity did Rose believe was her birth father?
   - (A) Cary Grant
   - (B) Charlie Chaplin
   - (C) Bob Hope
   - (D) W.C. Fields

5. What acclaimed actor portrayed Rose's biological father?
   - (A) Don Ameche
   - (B) Claude Akins
   - (C) Hume Cronyn
   - (D) Burgess Meredith

6. What actress played Sophia's sister,
   Angela?
   (A) Ruth Gordon
   (B) Ann Sothern
   (C) Nancy Walker
   (D) Lillian Gish

7. What game show did the Girls appear
   on together?
   (A) *Jeopardy*
   (B) *Grab That Dough!*
   (C) *Wheel of Fortune*
   (D) *Pig in a Poke*

8. Which two "celebrities" were
   pursuing Dorothy in Blanche's
   recurring dream?
   (A) Sonny Bono and Lyle
       Waggoner
   (B) Abbott & Costello
   (C) Tom Cruise and Mel Gibson
   (D) Ziegfried & Roy

9. St. Olaf, Rose's hometown, was located in which state?
   (A) Iowa
   (B) Wisconsin
   (C) Minnesota
   (D) North Dakota

10. What was the name of Dorothy's never-seen brother?
    (A) Hank
    (B) Phil
    (C) Chuck
    (D) Bob

11. By what name did Blanche always refer to her father?
    (A) Daddy Warbucks
    (B) Papa Bear
    (C) Father Dearest
    (D) Big Daddy

12. Rose was honored with which prestigious award?
   - (A) St. Olaf's Woman of the Year
   - (B) Nobel Peace Prize
   - (C) Miami Beach's Best Tap Dancer
   - (D) Blue Ribbon in Cow Insemination

13. Dorothy's brother practiced which fetish?
   - (A) S&M
   - (B) Cross-dressing
   - (C) Foot worship
   - (D) Judy Garland impersonator

14. After Dorothy's husband, Stan, divorced her, where did he live?
   - (A) Hawaii
   - (B) Arizona
   - (C) California
   - (D) Acapulco, Mexico

15. What was Rose's occupation at the beginning of the series?
    (A) Dairy farmer
    (B) Museum worker
    (C) Hospital volunteer
    (D) Grief counselor

16. Where was Blanche's place of employment?
    (A) Singles bar
    (B) Museum
    (C) Travel agency
    (D) Neiman-Marcus department store

17. Blanche and Rose kicked Dorothy out of which club?
    (A) Unofficial Elvis Fan Club
    (B) Tony Bennett Fan Club
    (C) Daughters of the Confederacy
    (D) The Shriners

18. Which actor portrayed an agoraphobic hippie, who Dorothy tried to help conquer his fears?
    - (A) Martin Sheen
    - (B) Peter Fonda
    - (C) Martin Mull
    - (D) Dennis Hopper

19. Dorothy suffered from which undiagnosed ailment?
    - (A) Chronic Fatigue Syndrome
    - (B) African Sleeping Sickness
    - (C) Krohn's Disease
    - (D) Mononucleosis

20. What did Blanche's daughter, Becky, name her baby girl?
    - (A) Charmaine
    - (B) Aurora
    - (C) Rainbow
    - (D) Shelby Lynne

21. What type of business did Sophia and her second husband, Max, open together?
   (A) Candy store
   (B) Bagel and lox shop
   (C) Pretzel stand
   (D) Pizza/knish stand

22. Whose concert did the Girls attend the night their home was burglarized?
   (A) Frank Sinatra
   (B) Madonna
   (C) Bobby Vinton
   (D) Tom Jones

23. What did Sophia's brother, Angelo, pretend to be?
   (A) Priest
   (B) Mafia hit man
   (C) Opera singer
   (D) Famous explorer

24. Who was the Girls' next-door neighbor?
    (A) Dr. Cliff Huxtable
    (B) George Jefferson
    (C) Sylvester Stallone
    (D) Dr. Harry Westin

25. Which US president paid a visit to the Girls?
    (A) Richard Nixon
    (B) Ronald Reagan
    (C) George Herbert Bush
    (D) Jimmy Carter

26. What animals did the Girls try to unsuccessfully breed?
    (A) Rabbits
    (B) Chinchillas
    (C) Minks
    (D) Horses

27. The Girls purchased a painting by what ailing artist?
    (A) Jasper de Kimmel
    (B) Jackson Pollack
    (C) Pablo Picasso
    (D) Andy Warhol

28. What celebrity bought the aviator's jacket that Sophia had accidentally placed a $10,000 winning lottery ticket in the pocket?
    (A) Neil Diamond
    (B) Elton John
    (C) Boy George
    (D) Michael Jackson

29. Who was Rose's long-time boyfriend?
    (A) Larry
    (B) Homer
    (C) Miles
    (D) Jebediah

30. What kiddie show host did Rose
    briefly date?
    (A) Mr. Terrific
    (B) Mr. Wonderful
    (C) Mr. Rogers
    (D) Captain Kangaroo

31. What was the name of Blanche's gay
    brother?
    (A) Jackson
    (B) Clayton
    (C) Jamie
    (D) George

32. What was the name of Rose's
    cherished, kidnapped teddy bear?
    (A) Teddy
    (B) Lorenzo
    (C) Fernando
    (D) Mr. Longfellow

33. With which world leader did Sophia claim to have an affair?
   (A) Winston Churchill
   (B) Benito Mussolini
   (C) Franklin Delano Roosevelt
   (D) Josef Stalin

34. Which pair of offspring had a casual affair?
   (A) Blanche's daughter Janet & Dorothy's son Michael
   (B) Blanche's son Skippy & Rose's daughter Gretchen
   (C) Rose's daughter Bridget & Blanche's son Doug
   (D) Rose's daughter Bridget & Dorothy's son Michael

35. Who did Dorothy claim to look like in photographs?
   (A) Karl Malden
   (B) Fess Parker
   (C) Ernest Borgnine
   (D) Chuck Connors

36. What was the name of Dorothy's pompous and bigoted novelist friend?
    (A) Barbara Thorndyke
    (B) Beatrice Woodiwiss
    (C) Serena Collinwood
    (D) Rosemary Steel

37. When Rose's Uncle Higenblotter died, who inherited the bulk of his estate?
    (A) His favorite cow, Betsy
    (B) Rose's mother
    (C) His prize-winning pig, Baby
    (D) Rose and her sister, Holly

38. Which show was a spin-off series of *The Golden Girls*?
    (A) *Amen*
    (B) *Empty Nest*
    (C) *227*
    (D) *Falcon Crest*

39. What role did Dorothy play in the grade-school production of *Henny Penny*?
    (A) Turkey Lurkey
    (B) Henny Penny
    (C) Goosey Loosey
    (D) Foxy Loxy

40. Who was eccentric artist Laszlo's inspiration for his sculpture?
    (A) Rose
    (B) Blanche
    (C) Dorothy
    (D) All of the above

41. What was the name of Blanche's college sorority?
    (A) The Alfa-Hos
    (B) The Alfa-Gamms
    (C) The Beta Zoids
    (D) The Southern Belles

42. Rose's longtime boyfriend was placed in the witness protection agency for testifying against which mobster?
(A) Mickey "The Cheeseman" Moran
(B) Bugsy Malone
(C) Don "The Fish" Grimaldi
(D) Lucky Luchavilla

43. According to Rose, what is a *videnfrugen?*
(A) Dairy maid
(B) Pig farmer's wife
(C) Servant
(D) Prostitute

44. Which actor portrayed Sophia's boyfriend, Rocco, a wannabe Mafia kingpin?
(A) Martin Landau
(B) Mickey Rooney
(C) Red Skelton
(D) Art Carney

45. Sophia claimed to be the former friend and business partner to which famous Italian chef?

    (A) Chef Boyardee

    (B) Tia Graziela

    (C) Papa John

    (D) Mama Celeste

46. When Stanley's Uncle Morris died, what did Dorothy and Stan inherit from him?

    (A) Apartment building

    (B) Small Caribbean island

    (C) Candy apple red '57 Chevy

    (D) A Pig

47. What did Blanche decide to do after attending her high school reunion?

    (A) Marry her old college flame Ham Lushbaum

    (B) Sell her home and move to Australia

    (C) Become a lesbian

    (D) Have a plastic surgery overhaul

48. What was the name of Blanche's girlhood home?

    (A) Four Magnolias

    (B) Skyhaven Farms

    (C) Tara

    (D) Twin Oaks

49. Rose suffered a heart attack while attending what function?

    (A) Her daughter Kirsten's wedding

    (B) A bogus class reunion

    (C) A funeral for her cat, Mr. Peepers

    (D) A fashion show

50. What type of doctor did Dorothy's daughter, Kate, marry?

    (A) Podiatrist

    (B) Gynecologist

    (C) Pediatrician

    (D) Proctologist

True or False

Answer the following True or False questions:

51. Estelle Getty is actually younger than Bea Arthur, who played her daughter on the show.

_____

52. Sophia's favorite pet name for Dorothy was "Bigfoot".

_____

53. Blanche's sister, Virginia, needed an emergency heart transplant to save her life.

_____

54. *The Golden Girls* was broadcast on Saturday nights on NBC throughout its entire run. _____

55. Blanche and Sophia once dated the same man simultaneously, a wealthy Cuban cigar exporter named Fidel Santiago.

_____

56. Sophia was accused of burning down the retirement home by leaving a fondue-chaffing dish on in her room overnight.

_____

57. Rose believed she saw a UFO that turned out to be a top-secret military experiment. _____

58. Blanche was having a pedicure when word of her husband's death reached her.

_____

59. Dorothy's lesbian friend, Jean, fell in love with Blanche while visiting Dorothy.

_____

60. Bea Arthur and Rue McClanahan starred together on the groundbreaking television series *Maude*. _____

61. Rose believed her gynecologist touched her inappropriately during a routine examination. _____

62. Blanche's full named is Blanche Elizabeth Devereaux. _____

63. The Girls' favorite midnight snack was chocolate chip cookies and ice cream.

_____

64. A fish wrapped in newspaper was left on the doorstep as a warning after Dorothy refused to pass the high school football player. _____

65. Rose's husband, Charlie, had a heart attack while making love to her.

_____

66. Blanche's pet name for herself was "peacock". _____

67. Sophia was chosen to star in a nationwide television commercial for a denture adhesive. _____

68. Blanche's daughter, Rebecca, became pregnant through artificial insemination.

_____

69. Sophia was hit in the head by a basketball at a Miami Heat game and pretended to have an injury for a phony insurance claim. _____

70. Dorothy's husband, Stan, left her for a stewardess named Chrissie who was half his age. _____

71. Charlie, Rose's husband, was a used car salesman. _____

72. Stan was a novelty salesman.

_____

73. Blanche had to have an electronic pacemaker implanted. _____

74. When Rose and Blanche took *Dirty Dancing* lessons, sexually uninhibited Blanche had a difficult time mastering the intricate dance movements.

_____

75. Rose was invited to visit China after writing a letter to the Chinese Premiere, Mao Tse Tung. _____

76. Sophia's old friends, Philamena and Dominic, arrived from Sicily believing that Dorothy had been switched at birth with their daughter, Gina. _____

77. Stan got Dorothy pregnant before being drafted to fight in the Vietnam War.

_____

78. The boxer that Sophia "bought" was actually studying to be a concert violinist.

_____

79. Sophia "accidentally" took the Pope's ring while he was on an official Papal visit to Miami. _____

80. Rose lost the neighbor's dog, Dreyfus, while taking care of him. _____

81. Rose's cousin Sven from Sweden fell
madly in love with Blanche while visiting
Rose in Miami before his arranged marriage.

_____

82. Dorothy was the only character who was
not a widow. _____

83. Dorothy once did a stand-up comedy
routine at a local nightclub.

_____

84. A beau of Blanche's once died while
sharing her bed. _____

85. Dorothy's son, Michael, married an
African-American woman considerably
older than he was. _____

86. All four of the actresses received at least one Emmy Award for their roles on the show. _____

87. Sophia once claimed to have had a tryst with passionate Spanish artist Pablo Picasso.
_____

88. Rose admitted to having an affair on Charlie. _____

89. Blanche felt she was falling in love with her brother-in-law, Jamie, who was the spitting image of her deceased husband, George. _____

90. Dorothy was a substitute Science/Physics teacher. _____

Golden Girls Knowledge Test

Answer the following questions about the show:

91. At what address did the *Golden Girls* reside? _____

92. What was the name of the Hispanic boxer that Sophia "purchased"?

_____

93. What was the profession of Rose's biological father? _____

94. Why were Dorothy, Rose and Blanche arrested before they were to attend a party for Burt Reynolds? _____

95. Which of Blanche's sisters wrote a trashy romance novel titled *Vixen: Story of a Woman?* _____

96. Who was in the audience at Sophia and Max Weinstock's wedding?

_____

97. What color did Blanche use to describe a feeling of uncertainty and fear?

_____

98. What was the name of the consumer reporter who hired Rose?

_____

99. What was the name of the fictitious pen pal Blanche and Dorothy invented to boost Rose's morale? _____

100. What song did the Girls sing to calm a cranky baby they were babysitting.

_____

101. By what name did Sophia refer to her daughter-in-law, Angela?

_____

102. What name did Dorothy and Lucas christen their lovemaking?

_____

103. Why didn't Rose get to attend her high school graduation?

_____

104. What was the name of St. Olaf's sister city? _____

105. What job did Dorothy's former student, Randy Becker, offer to her?

_____

106. What was the item that Blanche's Mammy, Viola Watkins, wanted from Blanche after her father passed away?

_____

107. What was Rose's maiden name?

_____

108. What did Sophia claim to be doing to cause her hernia, which required surgery?

_____

109. What was the name of Stanley's invention that could open up hot baked potatoes without burning your fingers?

_____

110. Blanche claimed to be the body double to what famous actress in the suspense thriller *Dressed to Kill*?

_____

111. What did Rose make the Girls promise to do after they each died?

_____

112. What did Stan's Czech cousin Magda say was the best thing about America?

_____

113. What was Sophia's favorite derogatory nickname for her ex-son-in-law, Stanley?

_____

114. What *small* detail did Rose neglect to mention to the Girls about her boyfriend, Dr. Jonathon Newman?

_____

115. Which one of the Girl's high school friends played a practical joke, faking her own death during a very competitive tennis match? _____

116. What secondary character from the show's pilot episode was written out?

_____

117. What was the "intimidating" nickname Dorothy's students gave to her?

_____

118. What inventive present did Rose give to Miles for his birthday?

_____

119. What famed psychic appeared to Rose during a dream? _____

120. Which two characters collaborated on a book, *Tooncers the Mediocre Tiger*?

_____

121. What was Blanche's creative gift for the Girls the Christmas it snowed in Miami?

_____

122. What comedic legend portrayed Dorothy's boyfriend, Ken, a lawyer who wanted to give up his career to follow his dream of being a circus clown?

_____

123. What item belonging to Blanche did Rose shoot when she thought someone was trying to break into the house?

_____

124. What was the name of the convict who escaped from prison to meet his pen pal, Blanche? _____

125. In the show's pilot episode, why didn't Blanche marry Harry?

_____

126. What was Dorothy and Sophia's favorite card game?

_____

127. What happened to the dress Blanche wore to a benefit dinner, which she planned to return to the store after wearing only once? _____

128. Who was Dorothy's first lover after her divorce from Stanley was finalized?

_____

129. What actor played Blanche's Uncle Lucas, who married Dorothy in the show's final episode? _____

130. What did the Girls exchange with the roof repairman for a new roof?

_____

131. Where did Blanche meet wheelchair-bound sports agent Ted Tanner?

_____

132. What act did Dorothy and Sophia imitate in the Shady Pines Mother/Daughter Beauty Contest?

_____

133. For what reason did Blanche's husband George "fake" his own death?

_____

134. Who was Blanche's favorite "stand-by" boyfriend? _____

135. What always happens to Rose when she attends a wedding?

_____

136. Why did Rose believe her husband Charlie had slept with Blanche?

_____

137. Which character's husband had an extra-marital affair, which produced an illegitimate son, David?

_____

138. How did Blanche always describe Dorothy in her letters to her Uncle Lucas?

_____

139. What title was bestowed upon Blanche the day her father passed away?

_____

140. Who pretended to be Korean exchange student Kim Fung-Toi at the class reunion?

_____

141. What did Rose suggest she and Miles do together to break their relationship out of a rut? _____

142. What play were Rose and Blanche rehearsing when the Hurricane hit Miami?

_____

143. What name did Rose give at the hospital when she had to have an HIV blood test? _____

144. What was the occupation of Dorothy's itinerant son, Michael?

_____

145. Who chauffeured the limousine that took Dorothy to her wedding to Lucas?

_____

146. Rose held a telethon to save what Miami landmark?

_____

147. What popular actress played Rose's blind sister, Lily?

_____

148. How did Blanche's mother-in-law always introduce her?

_____

149. What future star made a guest appearance on the show as Bobby, the young FBI agent who was shot while on a stakeout at the Girls' home?

_____

150. What was the name of the cat Rose gave away to the little boy the day she first met Blanche at the supermarket?

_____

151. In what type of car did Dorothy and Stan consummate their relationship?

_____

152. Dorothy wanted Stan's cousin Magda to read what two books?

_____

153. What was the name of Rose's mother?

_____

154. Which two characters worked together on a jingle to boost tourism in Miami?

_____

155. Which character temporarily joined a nunnery? _____

156. To which religious denomination did Blanche belong?

_____

157. Rose took Dorothy to what "childish" location to celebrate her birthday?

_____

158. What was political candidate Gil Kessler's big secret?

_____

159. What was the name of Blanche's "loose" young niece?

_____

160. What were the Girls protesting at the docks when they were arrested?

_____

Bonus Questions:

A) What was the name of the nasty neighbor Rose "killed"?

B) Rose believed Charlie was talking to her through what household appliance?

C) Why were both Dorothy and Stan arrested?

D) What type of party did Blanche have when the suave, English jewel thief stole her necklace?

E) What was the name of the girl who kidnapped Rose's teddy bear?

F) Where did Dorothy's sister Gloria live?

G) What "big" prize did the Girls win on the game show?

H) What was the name of Sophia's 1st husband?

I) What was the name of the piano-playing chicken placed in Rose's care?

J) What special nickname did Sal give his daughter, Dorothy?

K) What was the name of Blanche's favorite bar?

L) What was the name of the man Blanche's brother was "engaged" to marry?

M) What item allegedly belonging to Elvis did the fan club possess?

Who Said It?

Indicate who said each of the quotes listed:
Dorothy, Sophia, Rose or Blanche:

161. "It's so good, we named it!"

_____

162. "Not as much as you hurt my *oonie*."

_____

163. "Don't get hit in the face with a steam hammer, that can kill you."

_____

164. "Live from New York, it's Saturday Night!" _____

165. "Is that Ms. Lana Turner, arising from her morning toilette?"

_____

166. "Thank you, Sheena, Queen of the Slut People."

_____

167. "Thank you for the lovely prayer. Now shut up and get into bed…"

_____

168. "Why couldn't they put Tony Bennett and Tony Martin on the same bill? Oh, who am I kidding; there will never be another Woodstock."

_____

169. "She bit me first!"

_____

170. "Was she that tremendously fat woman with a wooden leg and a hairless cat named Cincinnati Jake?"

_____

171. "Everybody always likes me! They have to!"

_____

172. "The man in the blue suit at table five is impotent; bon appetite!"

_____

173. "I look like the mother of a *Solid Gold* dancer."

_____

174. "Not this time! I'm tired of being the Tonto of the group!"

_____

175. "I lost Butter Queen! Haven't I suffered enough?"

_____

176. "Oh, I do! I do believe in sluts!"

_____

177. "I'm a Grade A chucklehead."

_____

178. "You know, it was hard to get my Daddy angry. But once you did, he could be a real peckerwood."

_____

179. "Try ten days without a bowel movement sometime."

_____

180. "She has a cramp, you pea brain!"

_____

181. "To sleep, per chance to dream. My god! What a wonderful line!"

_____

182. "No, I'm going to sing a Negro spiritual."

_____

183. "Thank you. But hot water and oatmeal everyday takes most of the credit."

_____

184. "I have a question. When I order at Fung Chow's and say no MSG, do they put it in anyway?"

_____

185. "Get your bunny nose out of my butt."

_____

186. "[You want to have the baby] Here? So close to Cuba?"

_____

187. "Give me a break, you can't smell that from the hall!"

_____

188. "Buy? Sperm used to be free. It was all over the place!"

_____

189. "You haven't seen anything until you've seen a crazed cow."

_____

190. "Nothing you ever do is good enough for your parents. They just nag and nag and nag until you want to strangle them. But you don't, because you are in a hospital, with resuscitating equipment!"

_____

191. "I feel like I'm in the middle of some terrible dream. But I know it can't be a dream because there are no boy dancers."

_____

192. "No, that couldn't have been a UFO. UFOs only appear over open fields in Kentucky."

_____

193. "I'd love to get him on a couch made of rich, Corinthian leather."

_____

194. "I am the battered consumer. I drive a Gremlin, for God's sake!"

_____

195. "How could I? It always seemed to be over before I was even in the room."

_____

196. "I thought you were a cheap slut and you wore too much makeup. I was wrong. You don't wear too much makeup!"

_____

197. "I was boiling water to shrink the cyst on my backside, so I thought, what the Hell, I'll throw in some tea bags and make myself a hero!" _____

198. "You're just a great big pile of estrogen, aren't you?"

_____

199. "Forgive me for not having the rolling gait of a nymphomaniac."

_____

200. "I found out you can't give a sponge bath without a person's consent."

_____

201. "I maced myself right there in the police station! There I was, writhing in pain. They thought I was on angel dust!"

---

202. "Call your father and tell the dirt bag to come to the wedding."

---

203. "We'd better stick to her like a tight shirt on a sweaty farmhand."

---

204. "Where did you go to school? The University of Jupiter?"

_____

205. "God as my witness, I will never pick up a man again… in a library… on a Saturday…unless he's cute…and drives a nice car. Amen."

_____

206. "I don't know how he got her in that deck of cards. But, there she was, right after the Queen of Hearts. Is this your baby?"

_____

207. Let's face it. You and I are Yawn City, population two." _____

208. "You don't know how much you really love a man until you see him streaking toward the Earth, trying to grab a bird."

_____

209. "I always hold my breath when I greet a man. It thrusts my breasts forward."

_____

210. "That's why the brown bear and the field mouse can share their love and live together in harmony. Of course, they can't mate or the mouse would explode."

_____

211. "Back off! Not all of us are classified by the Navy as a friendly port!"

_____

212. "Can you believe that back-stabbing slut?"

_____

213. "So? Did you and Arnie play find the cannoli?"

_____

214. "I was the only girl in the fifth grade whose boyfriend had a fake ID."

_____

215. "No! We also know how to make love and sing opera."

_____

216. "Personally, I like to lay into a kid with a melon baller. It's got a nice weight to it."

_____

217. "Like the fatal blossom of the ginsum weed, I entice with my fragrance, but I can provide no succor."

----

218. "I'm going to have students that know Chekhov is a great, Russian playwright and not the navigator on the *Starship Enterprise.*"

----

219. "You once called my breasts perfect champagne glass sized orbs of dancing loveliness."

----

220. "I'd like to get excited, but I know no matter what happens, I'm going to get stuck cleaning out that peeing angel punch bowl."

---

221. "Did you just say 'I'm Mothra, giant radioactive insect… Reee!!! Reee!'?"

---

222. "I finally coaxed her out with a pork chop."

---

223. "I see little balls of sunshine in a bag."

---

224. "You're right. These naked, Southern boys sure can dance."

_____

225. "I can't put my finger on it just yet. But if I could, I'd have to wash it."

_____

226. "His campaign slogan was 'Vote for Me, I'll Show You My Wee-Wee'."

_____

227. "He's a priest, isn't he?"

_____

228. "Am I the only one here who feels like taking off all her clothes and doing the hokey pokey?"

_____

229. "You know how fragile men's egos are. One little mistake like screaming out the wrong name and they go all to pieces."

_____

230. "I promise to say 'Hail Mary' until Madonna has a hit movie."

_____

Bea, Betty, Estelle or Rue?

Below is a line or two describing one of the Golden Girls' accomplishments. Indicate which actress, Bea, Betty, Estelle or Rue, each statement applies to:

1. She co-starred on *Mama's Family* along with Vickie Lawrence.

   _____

2. This actress appeared on Broadway in the musical "Mame".

   _____

3. She played Sylvester Stallone's mother in the movie *Stop! Or My Mom Will Shoot*.

   _____

4. She starred on a successful spin-off
   series of *All In the Family*.

   _____

5. She is the youngest of the four actresses.

   _____

6. She was born in rural Oklahoma.

   _____

7. She played Yenta the Matchmaker in
   "Fiddler on the Roof"

   _____

8. This actress now suffers from Parkinson's Disease.

_____

9. She starred on the soap opera *Another World*.

_____

10. She earned her first Emmy Award in 1952.

_____

11. She recently had a lifesaving mastectomy.

_____

12. She has two adopted sons, Matthew and David.

_____

13. She played Harvey Fierstein's mother in "Torch Song Trilogy".

_____

14. She hosts a radio show about animals.

_____

15. She has won the most Emmy Awards.

_____

Classic Quotes…

* * *

Sophia [to Blanche]: "Jean is a lesbian."

Blanche: "What's funny about that?"

Sophia: "You aren't surprised?"

Blanche: "Of course not. I've never known any personally, but isn't Danny Thomas one?"

Dorothy: "Not Lebanese, Blanche, lesbian."

Blanche: "Lesbian? Lesbian? Lesbian! Isn't that one woman and another…"

Dorothy: "We know what it means, Blanche!"

***

Blanche: "Mel makes me feel young and beautiful and special. When we're together, we laugh a lot."

Sophia: "Why wouldn't you? You're both naked."

***

Rose [about St. Olaf]: "Ned was sort of the town idiot."

Sophia: "When? On your days off?"

***

Blanche: [talking about her brother]: "I don't really mind Clayton being homosexual. I just don't like him dating men."

Dorothy: "You really haven't grasped the concept of this gay thing yet, have you?"

Blanche: "There must be homosexuals who date women."

Sophia: "Yes, they're called lesbians!"

***

Blanche: "I tried giving up sex once."

Dorothy: "I guess you fell off the wagon!"

Sophia: "And onto a naval base!"

***

Dorothy: "Ma, you're lying!"

Rose: "Dorothy, be positive."

Dorothy: "Okay, I'm *positive* you're lying!"

***

[Rose and Dorothy have to share a bed]

Rose: "I want you to know that you're sleeping with a liar."

Dorothy: "I wouldn't worry about it, Rose. Most of the men I've slept with have been liars."

***

[Dorothy and Sophia are playing the word game Scrabble]

Dorothy: "Ma, 'disdam' is not a word."

Sophia: "It certainly is!"

Dorothy: "Okay, prove it. Use it in a sentence."

Sophia: "You're no good at disdam game!"

***

Rose: "Once, I read your diary."

Blanche: "You did what?"

Rose: "Well, it was an accident. You left it open on the kitchen table. I was twenty pages into it before I realized it wasn't a Sidney Sheldon novel."

***

[The girls are selecting a coffin at a funeral home]

Dorothy: "Well, Mr. Pfeiffer…"

Mr. Pfeiffer: "That's pronounced P-feiffer. The 'p' isn't silent."

Dorothy: "Well, uh, Mr. P-feiffer, we're arranging a funeral."

Mr. Pfeiffer: "Isn't that lovely? The three of you are planning ahead for mother."

Sophia: "Hey, P-feiffer, how would you like a punch in the p-face?"

***

Blanche: "I'm abhorred."

Sophia: "We know what you are, Blanche. I'm glad to finally hear you admit it."

Blanche: "Sophia, I said abhorred."

Sophia: "Abhorred, a slut, a tramp. It's all the same."

***

Dorothy: "How's the diet coming, Blanche?"

Blanche: "Oh, just fine. It's a piece of cake. A big ol' piece of chocolate cake. Smothered in whipped cream and coconut flakes. And a lobster!"

***

Blanche: "Look at the shameless way she's flirting with him. Disgusting!"

Rose: "You flirted with him."

Blanche: "I'm from the South. Flirting is part of my heritage."

Rose: "What do you mean?"

Dorothy: "Her mother was a slut, too."

***

[Blanche is dating a much-younger man]

Blanche: "This is strictly off-the-record, but Dirk is nearly five years younger than I am."

Dorothy: "In what, Blanche? Dog years?"

***

Rose: "Do you know that promotion I was up for at the counseling center? Well, I found out that I can't have it unless I become bilingual."

Blanche: "Oh, honey, don't do that. No job is worth having to date women."

Dorothy: "Bilingual, Blanche. It means speaking more than one language."

Blanche: "Oh! Why did I think it was something sexual?"

Dorothy: "Listen, Ma, we cannot afford a new TV. We're using the household money to repair the roof and repave the driveway."

Sophia: "Great! What am I supposed to do while every other old lady on the block is watching *Cosby*?"

Dorothy: "Well, you can sit in the new driveway and hope that an amusing black family drops by."

***

Dorothy: "Stan and I had very little marriage relations at all. I totally cut off his sex."

Rose: "You mean it grows back!"

Dorothy: "Yes, Rose. He's a lizard!"

***

Dorothy: "Rose, what are you listening to?"

Rose: "A relaxation tape. The sound of the rain is supposed to relax me."

Dorothy: "Is it working?"

Rose: "Not really. I keep worrying that I left my car windows down."

***

[Rose and Dorothy discuss seeing a UFO]

Rose: "Well, it wasn't a plane. Planes aren't that thin or that bright."

Dorothy: "Neither is Oprah Winfrey, but that doesn't make her a flying saucer."

***

[Dorothy is seeking Rose and Blanche's opinion of her outfit]

Dorothy: "Okay, girls, which goes better, the silver chain or the pearls?"

Rose: "The chain."

Blanche: "An amateur's mistake. Can't you see that the chain accentuates the many folds of that turkey-like neck?"

Rose: "Well, that may be, but the pearls draw attention to the non-existent bosom."

Blanche: "Yes, but the chain leads the eye even lower, to that huge spare tire jutting out over those square, manly hips."

Dorothy: "Why don't I just wear a sign that says 'Too Ugly to Live'?"

Blanche: "Fine. But what are you going to hang it from, the pearls or the chain?"

Dorothy: "Neither! I'm going to spray paint it on my hump!"

***

Dorothy: "You'll have to excuse my mother. She survived a slight stroke which left her, if I can be frank, a complete burden."

***

[Stan is trying to woo Dorothy through song]

Stan: "Is it working?"

Dorothy: "I don't think so."

Stan: "Then you leave me no other choice. I'll have to pull out the big gun!"

Dorothy: "You're wasting your time, Stan. I'm familiar with the big gun…"

***

Blanche: "When they put me in prison, I'll be brave. I can handle it!"

Rose: "Blanche, you don't understand! They'll put you in a *woman's* prison!"

Blanche: "Oh, god, no!"

***

Blanche: "I've decided what I'm going to use my bonus check money for!"

Dorothy: "What?"

Blanche: "I'm going to have my breasts enlarged!"

Rose: "Blanche, you're joking!"

Blanche: "Rose, breasts are back in fashion. Besides, what God didn't give me, Dr. Ira Rozensweig will! He's the Picasso of plastic surgery!"

Dorothy: "Just make sure he doesn't attach one to your forehead!"

***

Blanche: "I don't look right in American clothes. I have a more European physique."

Rose: "Oh, in Europe they have big butts, too?"

***

[A paranoid Rose has just shot Blanche's vase]

Dorothy: "What happened?"

Blanche [in shock]: "She shot my vase!"

Dorothy: "What are you doing shooting? Are you crazy?"

Rose: "I heard a noise! I thought it was the robbers!"

Sophia: "I lived eighty, eighty-one years. I survived two world wars, pneumonia, a stroke, two major operations. One night, I'll belch and Stable Mable here will blow my head off!"

* * *

[Regarding a local actress]

Rose: "I thought she was good in *The Diary of Anne Frank.*"

Dorothy: "Rose, please! During the entire second act, the audience kept screaming 'She's in the attic! She's in the attic!'"

* * *

Rose: "I've been on the phone for a half hour and you'll never guess what happened?"

Dorothy: "You realized you forgot to dial first?"

Rose: "No."

Blanche: "You were holding the receiver the wrong way?"

Rose: "No!"

Dorothy: "You were talking into the TV remote instead of the phone?"

Rose: "No!"

Blanche: "A shoe?"

Rose: "No, I'm not an idiot! Wait, the TV has a remote?"

* * *

Blanche: "I'm wound up tighter that a girdle on a Baptist minister's wife at an all-you-can-eat pancake breakfast!"

* * *

[The roof to the house is leaking]

Blanche: "Wait! Is that my Cabana Club beach towel?"

Rose: "You mean the one with the naked couple being swept up in the waves?"

Blanche: "Yes! You can't use this towel!"

Dorothy: "Please, Blanche, this is an emergency!"

Blanche: "No, I have too many fond memories attached to this towel!"

Dorothy: "Blanche, I'm in no mood to hear about the endless parade of sexual encounters you have experienced up and down the Florida coastline, with nothing but this towel between your hot flesh and the cold, wet sand!"

Blanche: "Dorothy, I brought my baby son Skippy home from the hospital in this towel."

Dorothy: "You're lying, Blanche!"

Blanche: "Damn, you're good!"

* * *

[Blanche and Dorothy are fighting]
Blanche: "Tramp!"
Dorothy: "I, I am a tramp? Blanche, have you heard the latest ad campaigns? See the World, Sleep with Blanche Devereaux! Join the Army, Be All You Can Be and Sleep with Blanche Devereaux! The Marines Are Looking for a Few Good Men Who Have NOT Slept with Blanche Devereaux!"
Blanche: "Just what are you trying to imply?"
Dorothy: "Slut!"
Blanche: "Trash!"
Rose: "Now girls, settle down before you say something you'll both regret."

* * *

Blanche: "What do you think I should do with my bed?"
Dorothy: "Put it in the Smithsonian, Blanche. It's got more miles on it than *The Spirit of St. Louis.*"

* * *

Dorothy: "After a while, you feel like you're in this gigantic, black hole."
Rose: "We had a gigantic black hole back in St. Olaf."
Sophia: "Oh, God!"
Rose: "Right in front of the courthouse where Charlie and I got our marriage license, and our permit to have kids. Oh, it was a lovely hole. Everybody in town would stand around and look into it."
Dorothy: "And they say Hollywood is the entertainment capital of the world."
Rose: "Well, we didn't just look. Sometimes, we'd point, too. Or spit and then time it. And then there was the guy who'd always unzip himself…"

* * *

Rose: "I would have died if I'd ever caught my parents having sex!"
Dorothy: "You never walked in on them?"
Rose: "Once. But they were only playing leap frog."
Sophia: "You walked in on your father and me once. Do you remember what I told you?"

Dorothy: "Yes. You said 'Mommy's sick; get help'!"

* * *

Dorothy: "Blanche, what's the matter?"
Blanche: "You know that attorney I've been dating? I just caught him handling melons at the A&P."
Dorothy: "And I take it they weren't yours?"

* * *

[Blanche and Dorothy have the flu]
Blanche: "Dorothy, where's my heating pad?"
Dorothy: "How should I know?"
Blanche: (pulling on an electrical cord) "If this isn't it, I'd like to know what other electrical appliance you're using under that blanket."

* * *

Rose: "Just because I'm built like this, you wouldn't believe how many people think I'm dumb."
Sophia: "Rose, you're too hard on yourself. I know people who think you are dumb over the phone."

* * *

Blanche: "Do you know what I hate doing the most after a party?"
Rose: "Trying to find your undies in the big pile?"
Blanche: "Cleaning up the dirty dishes, you twit!"

* * *

[Rose has just had open-heart surgery]
Blanche: "No one looks good after surgery, Sophia."
Sophia: "Try telling that to Cher."

Thank You for Being a Friend: The Golden Girls Trivia Answers

<u>Multiple Choice Answers:</u>

1. B, Shady Pines
2. D, Don Johnson
3. A, Hollingsworth
4. C, Bob Hope
5. A, Don Ameche
6. C, Nancy Walker
7. B, *Grab That Dough!*
8. A, Sonny Bono and Lyle Waggoner
9. C, Minnesota
10. B, Phil
11. D, Big Daddy
12. A, St. Olaf's Woman of the Year
13. B, Cross-dressing
14. A, Hawaii
15. D. Grief counselor
16. B, Museum
17. A, Unofficial Elvis Fan Club
18. C, Martin Mull

19. A, Chronic Fatigue Syndrome
20. B, Aurora
21. D, Pizza/knish stand
22. B, Madonna
23. A, Priest
24. D, Dr. Harry Westin
25. C, George Herbert Bush
26. C, Minks
27. A, Jasper de Kimmel
28. D, Michael Jackson
29. C, Miles
30. A, Mr. Terrific
31. B, Clayton
32. C, Fernando
33. A, Winston Churchill
34. D, Rose's daughter Bridget &
    Dorothy's son, Michael
35. B, Fess Parker
36. A, Barbara Thorndyke
37. C, His prize pig, Baby
38. B, *Empty Nest*

39. A, Turkey Lurkey
40. D, All of the Above
41. B, The Alfa-Gamms
42. A, Mickey "The Cheeseman" Moran
43. C, Servant
44. B, Mickey Rooney
45. D, Mama Celeste
46. A, Apartment building
47. D, Have a plastic surgery overhaul
48. D, Twin Oaks
49. B, A bogus class reunion
50. A, Podiatrist

<u>True or False Answers</u>

51. True, by two months
52. False. Sophia's favorite pet name for Dorothy was *Pussycat.*
53. False. She was in need of a kidney transplant.
54. True
55. True
56. False. Sophia was accused of leaving a hotplate on while making s'mores.
57. True
58. True
59. False. Jean thought she was falling in love with Rose.
60. True
61. False. It was her dentist who had "roaming hands".
62. True, making her initials *BED.*
63. False. If you didn't know the answer was cheesecake, Shame on you!
64. True
65. True.
66. False. She called herself "Water lily".
67. False. She was asked to be in a commercial for a pizza parlor.

68. True
69. False. She was "injured" during a baseball game she attended with Stanley and Dorothy.
70. True
71. False. He was a traveling insurance salesman.
72. True
73. True
74. True.
75. False. She was invited to Moscow after writing a letter to Soviet leader Mikhail Gorbachev.
76. True
77. False. Stanley was shipped off to Korea.
78. True, but Kid Pepe was studying to be a concert violinist.
79. True; it was later returned to the Pope.
80. False, Sophia misplaced Dreyfus.
81. True
82. True
83. True
84. False, but Rose did.

85. True
86. True
87. True
88. False
89. True
90. False, she was a substitute English teacher.

Golden Girls Knowledge Test Answers

91. 6151 Richmond Street, Miami Beach, Florida
92. Kid Pepe
93. He was a monk.
94. They were arrested during a prostitution sting.
95. Charmaine
96. A host of Elvis impersonators.
97. Magenta
98. Enrique Mas
99. Isaac Q. Newton
100. "Mr. Sandman"
101. Big Sally
102. Freddy Peterson
103. Rose contracted a nasty case of mononucleosis while manning a kissing booth and missed her graduation.
104. St. Gustav
105. He hired Dorothy to be a motivational speaker for his video game company, Borealis.
106. A music box she had given Big Daddy as a memento of their love affair.
107. Rose was adopted by the Lindstrom family.

108. Moving wicker furniture under Dorothy's orders. She actually helped place a car on blocks as a practical joke.
109. The Zborni
110. Ms. Angie Dickinson
111. To have their heads cryogenically frozen so they could be brought back to life.
112. Slurpees
113. Yutz!
114. He was a little person/dwarf.
115. Dorothy's competitive friend, Trudy.
116. Coco, the gay cook.
117. Attila the Sub
118. Sexy, boudoir photographs
119. The late Jean Dixon
120. Blanche and Rose; Rose later discovered the book had already been written by St. Olaf's most famous children's book author, Hans Christian Luckenhugen.
121. A calendar titled "The Men of Blanche's Boudoir"
122. Dick Van Dyke
123. Her Ming Vase
124. Merle Kellog
125. He was already married.
126. Gin rummy

127. Dorothy "accidentally" spilled orange juice on her dress.
128. Her divorce lawyer
129. Comedic genius Leslie Nielsen
130. A painting by Jasper de Kimmel
131. The library
132. Sonny and Cher
133. Trick question. In Blanche's recurring dream, George faked his own death to escape an overpowering debt.
134. Mel Bushman
135. She always "gets hot" at weddings.
136. She saw a double-exposed photograph of Charlie superimposed with one of Blanche on her bed.
137. Blanche
138. As that "Brooklyn Italian".
139. She was named "Citrus Ball Queen".
140. Rose
141. She suggested they go skydiving.
142. *The Sound of Music*
143. Dorothy Zbornak
144. A traveling jazz musician
145. Stanley

146. The McKinley lighthouse
147. Polly Holliday
148. "As George's 1st wife".
149. George Clooney
150. Mr. Peepers
151. A red, 1948 bullet-nosed Studebaker
152. Thomas Paine's *Common Sense* and Vanna White's autobiography
153. Alma Lindstrom
154. Rose & Dorothy
155. Sister Sophia
156. Blanche was a devout Southern Baptist.
157. Mr. Ha Ha's Hotdog Hacienda
158. "He" had been born a woman, Mary Anne Bonaduce.
159. Lucy
160. Tuna fishermen and their use of dragnets, which often kill innocent dolphins.

<u>Bonus Question Answers</u>

A) Mrs. Claxton
B) The refrigerator
C) For being slumlords
D) Moonlight Madness Party
E) Daisy
F) In a mansion in California
G) Electric skillet and a lifetime supply of soup
H) Guido Spirelli. It was an arranged marriage that Sophia later had annulled and married Dorothy's father, Salvador.
I) Count Bassy
J) Spumoni Face
K) The Rusty Anchor
L) Doug
M) A half-eaten pork chop, preserved in a glass case.

<u>Who Said It Answers</u>

161. Dorothy, about her lovemaking with Lucas.
162. Sophia, talking about the pain of giving birth to Dorothy.
163. Rose, recalling a near-death experience.
164. Rose, while heavily sedated before open-heart surgery.
165. Blanche, trying to sweet-talk Dorothy.
166. Sophia, to Blanche
167. Dorothy, pretending to be God to get Rose to shut up and go to bed.
168. Sophia
169. Sophia
170. Sophia, failing to recall an old neighbor.
171. Rose, upon discovering a co-worker doesn't like her.
172. Dorothy, when she finds out Stanley's brother Ted is a jerk, too.
173. Dorothy, to her date, a priest.
174. Sophia, feeling left out.
175. Rose, lamenting being in jail.
176. Dorothy, joyfully proclaiming her belief in Blanche.
177. Rose, stating the obvious.

178. Blanche, reminiscing about her idyllic Southern childhood.
179. Sophia, trying to one-up the Girls regarding physical discomfort.
180. Dorothy to Rose, during an aerobic workout.
181. Blanche, delirious from a severe lack of sleep.
182. Sophia.
183. Rose, on why she's always "consistent".
184. Sophia, to Dorothy's Chinese-American doctor.
185. Blanche, while sharing a bed with Rose, Dorothy and Sophia on a cold night.
186. Blanche, to her pregnant daughter.
187. Sophia.
188. Blanche.
189. Rose.
190. Dorothy, while in the hospital with her mother.
191. Blanche.
192. Dorothy to Rose, after witnessing strange lights in the night sky.
193. Blanche, about Rose's sexy new boss, Enrique Mas.

194. Rose, appealing to be hired for a new job.
195. Dorothy, referring to sex with Stanley.
196. Rose, about her first impressions of Blanche.
197. Sophia.
198. Dorothy to Blanche.
199. Dorothy, after Blanche criticizes the way she walks.
200. Blanche, on lessons learned.
201. Blanche, after spraying mace in her face at the police station.
202. Dorothy, to her daughter, Kate.
203. Blanche.
204. Dorothy to Blanche, about her outrageous weight claims.
205. Blanche, offering a prayer after picking up a married man in a library.
206. Rose, about a St. Olaf magician.
207. Rose, talking to Miles about their boring relationship.
208. Rose, after skydiving with Miles.
209. One of Blanche's many seduction tips.
210. Rose, mixing her metaphors during a protest.

211. Dorothy, to Blanche.
212. Rose, after Blanche agrees with her pleas to go out on a date with her boyfriend.
213. Sophia, when Rose returns home after a romantic cruise.
214. Blanche
215. Sophia, about Italians.
216. Sophia, dispensing advice on how to discipline a child.
217. Blanche, misunderstanding Dorothy's intentions.
218. Dorothy, happy to be teaching a gifted class.
219. Blanche, to sculptor Laszlo.
220. Dorothy
221. Sophia, denying she has a hearing problem.
222. Sophia, detailing how long she was in labor with Dorothy.
223. Blanche, with yet more delirious mutterings.
224. Dorothy, trying to lure Blanche from where she had handcuffed herself in her Grandmother's soon-to-be-demolished home.
225. Sophia, trying to uncover Gil Kessler's big secret.
226. Dorothy
227. Rose

228. Rose, getting "hot" during a wedding.
229. Blanche
230. Dorothy

Bea, Betty, Estelle or Rue Answers

1. Both Rue and Betty co-starred on *Mama's Family*.
2. Bea won a Tony Award for her performance in *Mame* in 1966.
3. Estelle
4. Bea and Rue were on the groundbreaking sitcom *Maude*.
5. Rue
6. Rue
7. Bea
8. Estelle
9. Rue
10. Betty
11. Rue
12. Bea
13. Estelle
14. Betty
15. Betty, with five Emmy wins.

<u>About the Author</u>

Michael D. Craig is the bestselling author of
*Thank You for Being a Friend: A Golden
Girls Trivia Book, Who's That Girl: The
Ultimate Madonna Trivia Book, The Totally
Awesome 80s Pop Music Trivia Book* and
The Totally Awesome 80s TV Trivia Book.
He lives in Kentucky and San Miguel de
Allende, Mexico, and is currently writing a
new work of non-fiction and running
Five Apples Press. You may contact him at
<u>AwritersHelper5@aol.com</u>.

<u>Epilogue</u>

"To me, The Golden Girls was always, in essence, about the strength of friendship, the power of humanity, the importance of family, the simplicity of laughter, the beauty of women, regardless of age, and the enduring hope that no matter what stage we are in life or our social standing, one can always find camaraderie in this world, and often in the least expected of places..."

Michael D. Craig